Ariel Books

**Andrews McMeel
Publishing**

Kansas City

GO FOR THE GOLD

THOUGHTS ON ACHIEVING
YOUR PERSONAL BEST

GO

FOR THE

GOLD

THOUGHTS ON ACHIEVING

YOUR PERSONAL BEST

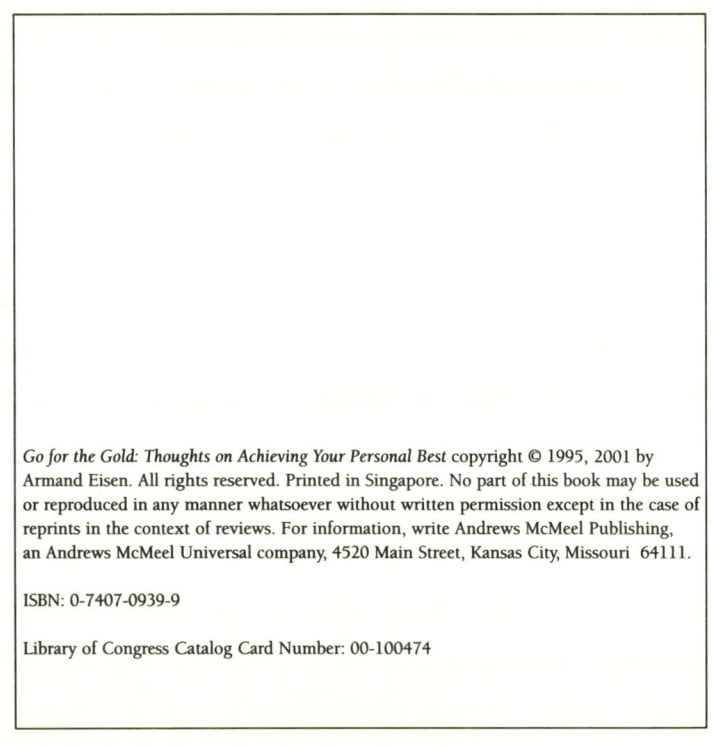

ISBN: 0-7407-0939-9

Library of Congress Catalog Card Number: 00-100474

CONTENTS

INTRODUCTION

We've all had times when we wanted to turn the car around, go back home, jump back into bed, and pull the covers up over our head. Our dreams, crystal clear to us the day before, suddenly appear obscured and out of reach. Abandoning our goal, we may busy ourselves with our daily routines for

a while. But very soon our inner voice will start clamoring to be heard. "Try again!" it says, "You can do it!" And so we pick ourselves up, brush ourselves off, and try again, finding we were closer to victory than we had first thought.

To live is to grow, and to grow is to experience life to the fullest. Take your singing out of the shower and into a concert hall. Plant the flower garden you always wanted. The important thing is to be an active participant in your life—not a spectator. Each of us is capable of doing something in a way no one else can. Finding out who we are and

what we want to do with our lives is a breathtaking adventure. And like most adventurers, we often have to brave the unknown to find what we seek.

Stretching our boundaries and continually challenging ourselves is a fascinating and fulfilling approach to life. Remember that setbacks are as common as successes on the way to the goal. What matters is pursuing your dream—whether it be packaging your own homemade tomato sauce, raising children, running a Fortune 500 company, or running a marathon. Take your dream off the shelf and go for it . . . ***go for the gold!***

Part I:
Taking Risks

Risk! Risk anything! Care no more
for the opinion of others,
for those voices. Do the hardest thing
on earth for you.
Act for yourself. Face the truth.

—Katherine Mansfield

Promote yourself but do not demote another.

—Israel Salanter

I say if it's going to be done, let's do it. Let's not put it in the hands of fate. Let's not put it in the hands of someone who doesn't know me. I know me best. Then take a breath and go ahead.

—Anita Baker

13

You are the architect
of your personal
experience.

—Shirley MacLaine

Don't be afraid to take a big

step if one is indicated.

You can't cross a chasm in

two small jumps.

—David Lloyd George

Follow your image as far
as you can no matter how
useless you think it is.
Push yourself.

—Nikki Giovanni

There's always room for improvement, you know —it's the biggest room in the house.

—Louise Heath Leber

17

I am only one; but still I am one.
I cannot do everything, but still
I can do something.
I will not refuse to do the
something I can do.

—Helen Keller

Life shrinks or
expands in
proportion to
one's courage.

—**Anaïs Nin**

You've got to get up every
morning with determination
if you're going to go to bed
with satisfaction.

—George Horace Lorimer

20

Whatever you attempt,
go at it with spirit.
Put some in!

—David Starr Jordan

I just go out and
do the best that
I can do.

—rookie pitcher
Wilson Alvarez

Keep in mind that
neither success nor
failure is ever final.

—Roger Babson

I do not want to die until I have faithfully made the most of my talent and cultivated the seed that was placed in me until the last small twig has grown.

—Käthe Kollwitz

First say to yourself
what you would be;
and then do what you
have to do.

—Epictetus

25

Better to strive and climb,
And never reach your goal,
Than to drift along with time—
An aimless, worthless soul,
Ay, better to climb and fall,
Or sow, though the yield be small,
Than to throw away day after day,
And never strive at all.

—Grace B. Hinkey

26

Above all, challenge yourself.
You may well surprise yourself at
what strengths you have, what
you can accomplish.

—Cecile M. Springer

A problem is a chance for you to do your best.

—Duke Ellington

I must tell you I take terrible risks. Because my playing is very clear, when I make a mistake you hear it. If you want me to play only the notes without any specific color dynamics, I will never make one mistake. Never be afraid to dare. And never imitate. Play without asking advice.

—Vladimir Horowitz

When it comes time to do your own life, you either perpetuate your childhood or you stand on it and finally kick it out from under.

—Rosellen Brown

It had long since come to my attention that people of accomplishment rarely sat back and let things happen to them. They went out and happened to *things*.

—Elinor Smith

We write our own
destiny. We become
what we do.

—Madame Chiang Kai-Shek

No one should negotiate their dreams. Dreams must be free to flee and fly high. No government, no legislature, has a right to limit your dreams. You should never agree to surrender your dreams.

—Reverend Jesse Jackson

The Wright brothers flew right through the smoke screen of impossibility.

—Charles F. Kettering

There is no such thing as *can't*, only *won't*. If you're qualified, all it takes is a burning desire to accomplish, to make a change. Go forward, go backward. Whatever it takes! But you can't blame other people or society in general. It all comes from your mind. When we do the impossible we realize we are special people.

—Jan Ashford

We cannot take anything for granted, beyond the first mathematical formula. Question everything else.

—**Maria Mitchell**

If the wind will
not serve, take to
the oars.

—Latin proverb

One never notices what has

been done; one can only see

what remains to be done.

—Marie Curie

You really *can* change the world if you care enough.

—Marian Wright Edelman

I sometimes say that success just happens. That's not true. You have to make it happen. When I make up my mind to do something, I make sure it happens. You can't wait for the phone to ring. You have to ring them.

—Lord (Lew) Grade

Age quid agis, says the Latin:
Do what you do. Be in
earnest, and do not trifle.

—C. H. Spurgeon

Knock the *t* off
the *can't*.

—George Reeves

Peace, like every other
rare and precious thing,
doesn't come to you. You
have to go and get it.

—Faith Forsyte

Your adrenaline has to run. Whatever business you are in, if you don't feel exhilarated by achieving your objectives and excelling in what you're doing, then you will never do very much well. You can do a lot of things competently. But you have to have a sense of being turned on by the thought of making something go well. It's doing something better than it has ever been done before, or creating a new refinement in what you're making or a better service than the other guy. This is how you build a business.

—Malcolm Forbes

44

Tomorrow's life is
too late. Live today.

—Martial

I am suffocated and lost
when I have not the
bright feeling of progression.

—Margaret Fuller

Pursue worthy aims.

—Solon

The time when you need to do something is when no one else is willing to do it, when people are saying it can't be done.

—Mary Frances Berry

Don't wait for your "ship to come in," and feel angry and cheated when it doesn't. Get going with something small.

—Irene Kassorla

In the long run men hit only what they aim at. Therefore, though they should fail immediately, they had better aim at something high.

—Henry David Thoreau

It doesn't matter how
much milk you spill
so long as you
don't lose the cow.

—Saying

The biggest temptation is . . . to settle for too little.

—Thomas Merton

I have always had a
dread of becoming a
passenger in life.

—Queen Margreth II of Denmark

To find in ourselves what makes life worth living is risky business, for it means that once we know we must seek it. It also means that without it life will be valueless.

—Marsha Sinetar

Whatever your sex or position, life is a battle in which you are to show your pluck, and woe be to the coward. Whether passed on a bed of sickness or a tented field, it is ever the same fair play and admits no foolish distinction. Despair and postponement are cowardice and defeat. Men were born to succeed, not to fail.

—Henry David Thoreau

Just go out there
and do what you've
got to do.

—**Martina Navratilova**

Yesterday I dared
to struggle. Today
I dare to win.

—Bernadette Devlin

Always remember what you're good at and stick with it.

—**Ermenegildo Zegna**

58

First, when everybody tells you that you are being idealistic or impractical, consider the possibility that everybody could be wrong about what is right for you. Look inside yourself the way nobody else can. Will the pursuit of your dream hurt anybody? Do you stand at least a fair chance of success? If you fail, will you be seriously damaged or merely embarrassed? If you succeed, will it change your life for the better? When you can persuade yourself that your dream is worthwhile and achievable—then say thank you to the doubters and take the plunge . . . How much better to know that we have dared to live our dreams than to live our lives in a lethargy of regret.

—Gilbert E. Kaplan

Do not wait for leaders; do it alone, person to person.

—Mother Teresa

60

Life is to be lived. If you have to support yourself, you had bloody well better find some way that is going to be interesting. And you don't do that by sitting around wondering about yourself.

—Katharine Hepburn

If you stand up and be counted, from time to time you may get yourself knocked down. But remember this: A man flattened by an opponent can get up again. A man flattened by conformity stays down for good.

—Thomas J. Watson, Jr.

Carpe diem, quam minimum credula a postero.

Seize the day, and put the least possible trust in tomorrow.

—Horace

Adventure is
worthwhile
in itself.

—Amelia Earhart

If you would attain to what you are not yet, you must always be displeased by what you are. For where you were pleased with yourself there you have remained. But once you have said, "It is enough," you are lost. Keep adding, keep walking, keep advancing; do not stop, do not turn back, do not turn from the straight road.

—St. Augustine

65

Everyone has talent. What is rare is the courage to follow the talent to the dark place where it leads.

—Erica Jong

In order to live . . . act;

in order to act . . .

make choices . . .

—**Ayn Rand**

That's the risk you take
if you change: that people you've
been involved with won't like
the new you. But other people
who do will come along.

—Lisa Alther

Love has nothing to do with
what you are expecting to get—
only with what you are expecting
to give—which is everything.

—Katharine Hepburn

Let us resolve to be masters, not the victims, of our history, controlling our own destiny without giving way to blind suspicions and emotions.

—John F. Kennedy

70

Have the courage
to act instead
of react.

—Earlene Larson Jenks

I have fought and kicked and fasted and prayed and cursed and cried myself to the point of existing. It has been like being born again, literally. Just *knowing* has meant everything to me. Knowing has pushed me out into the world, into college, into places, into people.

—Alice Walker

Men must live
and create.
Live to the point
of tears.

—Albert Camus

If we are afraid of that which is high, we shall end by giving a good imitation of ourselves; and of all forms of plagiarism, self-plagiarism is the worst.

—W. B. J. Martin

Take a chance! All life is a chance. The man who goes farthest is generally the one who is willing to do and dare.

—Dale Carnegie's scrapbook

Courageous risks are life
giving, they help you grow,
make you brave and better
than you think you are.

—Joan L. Curcio

We become just by performing just actions, temperate by performing temperate actions, brave by performing brave actions.

—Aristotle

It is better to die on your feet than to live on your knees.

—Dolores Ibarruri

I've always tried to go a step past wherever people expected me to end up.

—Beverly Sills

Do not follow where the
path may lead. Go
instead where there is
no path and leave a trail.

—Muriel Strode

To do something better, you must work an extra bit harder. I like the phrase an *extra bit harder.* For me it is not just a slogan, but a habitual state of mind, a disposition. Any job one takes on must be grasped and felt with one's soul, mind and heart; only then will one work an extra bit harder.

—Mikhail Gorbachev

You can't always expect
a certain result, but
you can expect to
do your best.

—Anita Hill

You can do what you have to do, and sometimes you can do it even better than you think you can.

—Jimmy Carter

One can never consent
to creep when one feels
an impulse to soar.

—Helen Keller

Become a possibilitarian. No matter how dark things seem to be or actually are, raise your sights and see the possibilities—always see them, for they're always there.

—Norman Vincent Peale

85

You might as well live.

—Dorothy Parker

I'm the foe of moderation, the champion of excess. If I may lift a line from a diehard whose identity is lost in the shuffle, "I'd rather be strongly wrong than weakly right."

—Tallulah Bankhead

87

Nothing would be done
at all if a man waited till he
could do it so well that no
one could find fault with it.

—Cardinal Newman

At the root of human responsibility is the concept of perfection, the urge to achieve it, the intelligence to find a path towards it, and the will to follow that path, if not to the end at least the distance needed to rise above individual limitations and environmental impediments.

—Aung San Suu Kyi

Do noble things,
do not dream them
all day long.

—Charles Kingsley

I could not, at any age, be content to take my place in a corner by the fireside and simply look on. Life was meant to be lived. Curiosity must be kept alive. The fatal thing is the rejection. One must never, for whatever reason, turn his back on life.

—Eleanor Roosevelt

Don't give up. Keep going. There is always a chance that you will stumble onto something terrific. I have never heard of anyone stumbling over anything while he was sitting down.

—Ann Landers

You have to . . . learn the rules of the game. And then you have to play better than anyone else.

—Dianne Feinstein

Be not simply good;
be good for something.

—Henry David Thoreau

I have never wanted to be anything but a gymnast. Maybe it is dangerous—but when you start thinking of danger, you might as well give up.

—Olga Korbut

There are two ways of meeting difficulties: You alter the difficulties or you alter yourself to meet them.

—Phyllis Bottome

We must dare,
and dare again,
and go on daring.

—Georges Jacques Danton

You do what you can for as long as you can, and when you finally can't, you do the next best thing. You back up but you don't give up.

—Charles "Chuck" Yeager

. . . I can do what I want to do and that has been my greatest gift.

—Faith Ringgold

This became a credo of mine: attempt the impossible in order to improve your work.

—Bette Davis

Just don't give up trying to do
what you really want to do.
Where there is love and
inspiration, I don't think
you can go wrong.

—Ella Fitzgerald

We have to dare to be
ourselves, however frightening
or strange that self may
prove to be.

—May Sarton

When you do nothing, you feel overwhelmed and powerless. But when you get involved, you feel the sense of hope and accomplishment that comes from knowing you are working to make things better.

—Pauline R. Kezer

Struggle and survival, losing and winning, doesn't matter. It's entering the race that counts. You enter, you can win, you can lose . . . but it's all about entering the race.

—Pam Grier

The ripest peach is

highest on the tree.

—James Whitcomb Riley

I think it's the end of progress
if you stand still and think
of what you've done in
the past. I keep on.

—**Leslie Caron**

Choose to have a career early and a family late. Or choose to have a family early and a career late— but plan a long life.

—Dr. Janet Davison Rowley

Don't be afraid to give
up the good to go
for the great.

—Kenny Rogers

[There] is a need to find and sing our own song, to stretch our limbs and shake them in a dance so wild that nothing can roost there, that stirs the yearning for solitary voyage.

—Barbara Lazear Ascher

As time passes we all get
better at blazing a trail
through the thicket of advice.

—Margot Bennett

The idea is to win, you win the way you have to. Sometimes it's a good idea to save all your energy for the really tough battles.

—Sugar Ray Robinson

To hit mark, aim
above it.

—**Anonymous**

You were once wild
here. Don't let
them tame you!

—Isadora Duncan

113

I praise loudly;
I blame softly.

—Catherine II

The cards you hold in the
game of life mean very little—
it's the way you play
them that counts.

—Saying

There are people who put their dreams in a little box and say, "Yes, I've got dreams, of course, I've got dreams." Then they put the box away and bring it out once in a while to look in it, and yep, they're still there. These are *great* dreams, but they never even get out of the box. It takes an uncommon amount of guts to put your dreams on the line, to hold them up and say, "How good or how bad am I?" That's where courage comes in.

—**Erma Bombeck**

He that leaveth nothing to chance will do few things ill, but he will do very few things.

—George Savile

What's terrible is to pretend that the second-rate is first-rate. To pretend that you don't need love when you do; or you like your work when you know quite well you're capable of better.

—Doris Lessing

Thomas Carlyle was once talking to a young friend, and asked him what his aim in life was. The young man replied that he had none. "Get one, then, and get it *quick*," said Carlyle, sharply. "Make something your specialty. Life is a very uncertain affair. Knowing a little about five hundred things won't do us much good. We must be able to do something well, that our work will be needed and valuable."

—Kate L. Gates

Nothing that is beautiful
is easy, but everything
is possible.

—Mercedes de Acosta

Don't wait for your ship to come; swim out to it.

—Anonymous

As long as you're going to think anyway, think big.

—Donald Trump

Never change a winning game; always change a losing one.

—Bill Tilden

If you obey all
the rules you miss
all the fun.

—Katharine Hepburn

I learned certain things about wasting energy. It hit me the hardest after the French [Open, which he lost]. The important thing is to learn a lesson every time you lose. Life is a learning process and you have to try to learn what's best for you. Let me tell you, life is not fun when you're banging your head against a brick wall all the time.

—John McEnroe

125

Mama exhorted her children at every opportunity to "jump at de sun." We might not land on the sun, but at least we would get off the ground.

—Zora Neale Hurston

The good that Martin Luther King Jr. did remains undiminished . . . He was great precisely because, like other heroes, he did not allow human weakness to deter him from doing great works.

—Carl McClendon

Face your deficiencies and acknowledge them; but do not let them master you. Let them teach you patience, sweetness, insight.... When we do the best we can, we never know what miracle is wrought in our life, or in the life of another.

—Helen Keller

I've hit 755 home runs, and I did it without putting a needle in my arm or a whiskey bottle in my mouth.

—**Hank Aaron**

I think that wherever your journey takes you, there are new gods waiting there, with divine patience— and laughter.

—Susan M. Watkins

It was a high counsel
that I once heard given to
a young person, "Always
do what you are
afraid to do."

—Ralph Waldo Emerson

While others may argue about whether the world ends with a bang or a whimper, I just want to make sure mine doesn't end with a whine.

—Barbara Gordon

The world has no room for cowards. We must all be ready somehow to toil, to suffer, to die. And yours is not the less noble because no drum beats before you when you go out into your daily battlefields, and no crowds shout about your coming when you return from you daily victory or defeat.

—Robert Louis Stevenson

It is necessary to try to pass one's self always; this occupation ought to last as long as life.

—Queen Christina of Sweden

134

We don't know who
we are until we see
what we can do.

—Martha Grimes

. . . **b**e not afraid of greatness: some are born great, some achieve greatness, and some have greatness thrust upon them.

—**William Shakespeare**

Let a man who has to make his fortune in life remember this maxim: Attacking is the only secret. Dare and the world always yields; or if it beats you sometimes, dare it again and it will succumb.

—William Makepeace Thackeray

Happy people plan actions, they don't plan results.

—Dennis Wholey

And whatsoever ye do, do it heartily.

—Colossians 3:23

When you can't solve the problem, manage it.

—Robert H. Schuller

Our grand business in life is
not to see what lies dimly at
a distance, but to do what
lies clearly at hand.

—Thomas Carlyle

Nothing in life is to be feared. It is only to be understood.

—Marie Curie

If you once turn on your side after the hour at which you ought to rise, it is all over. Bolt up at once.

—Sir Walter Scott

The excitement, the true excitement, was always in starting again. Nothing's worse than an accomplished task, a realized dream.

—**Marilyn Harris**

Never trouble another for what you can do for yourself.

—Thomas Jefferson

I am a great believer in luck, and I find the harder I work the more I have of it.

—Stephen Butler Leacock

146

Living at risk is jumping off the cliff and building your wings on the way down.

—Ray Bradbury

See into life—don't
just look at it.

—Anne Baxter

If you want your
dreams to come true,
don't sleep.

—Yiddish proverb

Just keep going.
Everybody gets better if
they keep at it.

—Ted Williams

Shoot for the moon.
Even if you miss it you
will land among the stars.

—Les Brown

There is nothing wrong in admitting you are afraid. But whenever something threatens you, instead of running away, hold your ground and repeat the mantra **Rama**, Rama [God, God] over and over again in your mind. It can turn your fear into fearlessness.

—advice of an old family servant to Mohandas K. Gandhi

In order to succeed, at times you have to make something from nothing.

—Ruth Mickleby-Land

From a certain point onward there is no longer any turning back. That is the point that must be reached.

—Franz Kafka

The dedicated life is the life worth living. You must give with your whole heart.

—Annie Dillard

If I could get the ear of every young man but for one word, it would be this; make the most and **best** of yourself. There is no tragedy like a wasted life—a life failing of its true end, and turned to a false end.

—T. T. Munger

156

I can't imagine a person becoming a success who doesn't give this game of life everything he's got.

—Walter Cronkite

Nothing liberates our greatness like the desire to help, the desire to serve.

—Marianne Williamson

Strange that any human being should be content with less than the fullness of life! I take that back. We are not content to be less than we might be, but at times we do fail in courage, or we become tired and need a hand on our shoulder to hearten us. I need it often. When my spirits are a bit low, I give myself Goethe's advice: "Remember to live."

—John Erskine

It had been my repeated experience that when you said to life calmly and firmly (but very firmly!), "I **trust** you; do what you must," life had an uncanny way of responding to your need.

—Olga Ilyin

The wonder is what
you can make a
paradise out of.

—Eva Hoffman

Don't bunt. Aim out of the ball park. Aim for the company of the immortals.

—David Ogilvy

If you shut your door
to all errors, truth
will be shut out.

—Rabindranath Tagore

Adhere to your own act, and congratulate yourself if you have done something strange and extravagant, and broken the monotony of a decorous age.

—Ralph Waldo Emerson

Striving for excellence
motivates you; striving for
perfection is demoralizing.

—Dr. Harriet Braiker

There is no meaning to life except the meaning man gives his life by the unfolding of his powers, by living productively.

—Erich Fromm

Cultivate your garden . . . Do not depend upon teachers to educate you . . . follow your own bent, pursue your curiosity bravely, express yourself, make your own harmony . . . In the end, education, like happiness, is individual, and must come to us from life and from ourselves. There is no way; each pilgrim must make his own path. "Happiness," said Chamfort, "is not easily won; it is hard to find it in ourselves, and impossible to find it elsewhere."

—Will Durant

Let me win, but if I cannot win, let me be brave in the attempt.

— **Special Olympics motto**

. . . **W**hatever you can do or dream you can, begin it. Boldness has genius, power and magic in it. Begin it now.

—Goethe, attributed

. . . there is no prescribed route to follow to arrive at a new idea. You have to make the intuitive leap. But the difference is that once you've made the intuitive leap you have to justify it by filling in the intermediate steps. In my case, it often happens that I have an idea, but then I try to fill in the intermediate steps and find that they don't work, so I have to give it up.

—Stephen W. Hawking

There is no point at which you can say, "Well, I'm successful now. I might as well take a nap."

—Carrie Fisher

Life is either a daring adventure or nothing.

—Helen Keller

To strive, to seek,
to find, and not
to yield.

—Alfred, Lord Tennyson

Plunge boldly into
the thick of life!

—Johann Wolfgang
von Goethe

N

ever go backward.
Attempt, and do it with
all your might.
Determination is power.

—Charles Simmons

If you really want to be happy, nobody can stop you.

—Sister Mary Tricky

What I want to tell you today is not to move into that world where you're alone with yourself and your mantra and your fitness program or whatever it is that you might use to try to control the world by closing it out. I want to tell you just to live in the mess. Throw yourself out into the convulsions of the world. I'm not telling you to make the world better, because I don't believe progress is necessarily part of the package. I'm telling you to live in it. Try and get it. Take chances, make your own work, take pride in it. Seize the moment.

—Joan Didion

177

Ride on! Rough-shod if need be, smooth-shod if that will do, but ride on! Ride on over all obstacles, and win the race!

—Charles Dickens

To improve the golden
moment of opportunity, and
catch the good that is within
our reach, is the great
art of life.

—**William James**

Well done is better than than well said.

—Benjamin Franklin

If you cannot win, you *must* win.

—Maxim of Reb Menshim Mendl of Kotsk

This one thing I do, forgetting those things which are behind, and reaching forth unto those things which are before.

—Philippians 3:13

I might have been born in a hovel, but I determined to travel with the wind and the stars.

—Jacqueline Cochran

183

Remember, you can't steal second if you don't take your foot off first.

—Mike Todd

Having a dream isn't stupid, Norm. It's not having a dream that's stupid.

—Cliff Clavin, "Cheers"

Fight hard when you are down; die hard—determine at least to do—and you won't die at all.

—**James H. West**

When fog prevents a small-boat sailor from seeing the buoy marking the course he wants, he turns his boat rapidly in small circles, knowing that the waves he makes will rock the buoy in the vicinity. Then he stops, listens and repeats the procedure until he hears the buoy clang. By making waves, he finds where his course lies . . . Often the price of finding these guides is a willingness to take a few risks, to "make a few waves." A boat that stays in the harbor never encounters danger—but it also never gets anywhere. "Put out into deep water." (New Testament, Luke 5:4)

—Richard Armstrong

187

The difficult we do immediately; the impossible takes a little longer.

—slogan of the United States Army Service Forces

Never, never, never, never give up.

—Winston Churchill

Take risks . . . be willing to put your mind and your spirit, your time and your energy, your stomach and your emotions on the line. To search for a safe place, to search for an end to a rainbow, is to search for a place that you will hate once you find it. The soul must be nourished along with the bank account and the résumé. The best nourishment for any soul is to create your own risks.

—Jim Lehrer

Demand the best from yourself, because others will demand the best of you. . . . Successful people don't simply give a project hard work. They give it their best work.

—Win Borden

To strive, to seek,
to find, and
not to yield.

—Alfred, Lord Tennyson

Next to being what we ought to be, the most desirable thing is that we should become what we ought to be as fast as possible.

—Herbert Spencer

You can be an ordinary athlete by getting away with less than your best. But if you want to be a great, you have to give it all you've got—your everything.

—Duke P. Kahanamoku

How to hit home runs: I swing as hard as I can, and I try to swing right through the ball. In boxing, your fist usually stops when you hit a man, but it's possible to hit so hard that your fist doesn't stop. I try to follow through in the same way. The harder you grip the bat, the more you can swing it through the ball, and the farther the ball will go. I swing big, with everything I've got. I hit big or I miss big. I like to live as big as I can.

—George Herman "Babe" Ruth

'**T**is better to have
fought and lost, than never
to have fought at all.

—**Arthur Clough**

Be bold. If you're going to

make an error, make a

doozy, and don't be afraid

to hit the ball.

—Billie Jean King

Whatever you do, do it to the purpose; do it **thoroughly**, not superficially. Go to the bottom of things. Any thing half done, or half known, is, in my mind, neither done nor known at all. Nay, worse, for it often misleads.

—Lord Chesterfield

Whatever you do, you should want to be the best at it. Every time you approach a task, you should be aiming to do the best job that's ever been done at it and not stop until you've done it. Anyone who does that will be successful—and rich.

—David Ogilvy

Act as if it were impossible to fail.

—Dorothea Brand

Do not hover always on the surface of things, nor take up suddenly, with mere appearances; but penetrate into the depth of matters, as far as your time and circumstances allow, especially in those things which relate to your own profession.

—Isaac Watts

You don't learn to hold your own in the world by standing on guard, but by attacking and getting well hammered yourself.

—George Bernard Shaw

We must dare to think unthinkable thoughts.

—James W. Fulbright

To a young man learning to perform on the flying trapeze a veteran circus performer once said: "Throw your heart over the bars and your body will follow." In every field of endeavor those who put their **hearts** in their work are the real leaders . . . Falling in love with one's job is the secret of success.

—Frat

Either lead, follow, or get out of the way.

—sign on desk of broadcasting executive Ted Turner

Whatever you do, put romance and enthusiasm into the life of our children.

—Margaret Ramsey MacDonald

You have to invest yourself. There are no nine-to-five possibilities in terms of true success in business or the professions. Dedication is the key.

—Jack Hilton

207

Those who love deeply never grow old; they may die of old age, but they die young.

—Sir Arthur Wing Pinero

They never told me I couldn't.

—Tom Dempsey

There's not a cliff too awesome
nor a stream too swift or deep,
Nor a haunted hill too eerie,
nor a mountain trail too steep
For the questing heart to venture
or the eager breath to dare.

—Lorraine Usher Babbitt

Never say
die.

—Charles Dickens

Every man is enthusiastic at times. One man has enthusiasm for thirty minutes, another has it for thirty days—but it is the man that has it for thirty years who makes a success in life.

—THE CATHOLIC LAYMAN

Somebody said that it couldn't be done,
But he with a chuckle replied
That "maybe it couldn't," but he would be one
Who wouldn't say so till he'd tried.
So he buckled right in with the trace of a grin
On his face. If he worried he hid it.
He started to sing as he tackled the thing
That couldn't be done, and he did it.

—Edgar A. Guest

To sense the potential of posterity in one's daily business life, one has to feel deeply about some aspect of one's work. One has to be **committed** to do or create something that will accomplish some good in this world . . . The key ingredients are dedication to a profound idea and the determination to carry it out.

—David Finn

214

The first rule is to keep an untroubled spirit. The second is to look things in the face and know them for what they are.

—Marcus Aurelius

Whatever I engage
in, I must push
inordinately.

—Andrew Carnegie

Attempt the impossible in order to improve your work.

—Bette Davis

To live each day as though one's last, never flustered, never apathetic, never attitudinizing—here is the perfection of character.

—Marcus Aurelius

218

Be wicked, be brave, be drunk, be reckless, be dissolute, be despotic, be an anarchist, be a suffragette, be anything you like—but for pity's sake be it to the top of your bent.

—Violet Trefusis

The first duty of a human being is to assume the right relationship to society—more briefly, to find your real job, and do it.

—**Charlotte Perkins Gilman**

It is not the critic who counts; not the man who points out how the strong man stumbles, or where the doer of deeds could have done better. The credit belongs to the man who is actually in the arena; whose face is marred by dust and sweat; who strives because there is no effort without errors and shortcomings, but does actually strive to do the deeds; who does know the great enthusiasm, the great devotion; who spends himself in a worthy cause; who at best, knows in the end the triumph of achievement, and who at the worst, if he fails, at least fails while daring greatly, so that his place shall never be with those cold and timid souls who know neither victory nor defeat.

—Theodore Roosevelt

Make the most of
yourself for that is
all there is to you.

—Ralph Waldo Emerson

The only place where success comes before work is in a dictionary.

—Vidal Sassoon

Keep strong if possible; in any case keep cool.

—Sir Basil Liddell

I don't think of myself as a poor deprived ghetto girl who made good. I think of myself as somebody who from an early age knew I was responsible for myself, and I had to make good.

—Oprah Winfrey

To laugh is to risk appearing the fool.

To weep is to risk appearing sentimental.

To reach for another is to risk involvement.

To expose your feelings is to risk exposing your true self.

To place your ideas, your dreams before a crowd
is to risk their loss.

To love is to risk not being loved in return.

To live is to risk dying.

To believe is to risk despair.

To try is to risk failure.

But risks must be taken, because the greatest hazard
in life is to risk nothing.

The person who risks nothing, does nothing, has
nothing, is nothing.

They may avoid suffering and sorrow, but they cannot
learn, feel, change, grow, love, live.

Chained by their attitudes they are slaves; they have
forfeited their freedom.

Only a person who risks is free.

—Anonymous Chicago teacher

You must learn day by day, year by year, to broaden your horizon. The more things you love, the more you are interested in, the more you enjoy, the more you are indignant about—the more you have left when anything happens.

—Ethel Barrymore

Go! Go! Go! It makes no difference where, just so you go! Go! Go! Remember at the first opportunity—go!

—Jeannette Rankin

There's only one way to succeed in anything, and that is to give it everything. I do, and I demand that my players do.

—Vince Lombardi

Life is either a daring
adventure or nothing at all.
Security is mostly a
superstition. It does not
exist in nature.

—Helen Keller

230

Part II:
Ingredients for Success

Nothing in life is to be feared.

It is only to be understood.

—Marie Curie

If you practice an art, be proud of it and make it proud of you . . . It may break your heart, but it will fill your heart before it breaks it; it will make you a person in your own right.

—Maxwell Anderson

People need to feel better about themselves, to feel that, yes, they can do it. First you think highly of yourself; then you accelerate.

—Janet Norflett

Keep company with those who may make you better.

—English saying

Life is a succession of moments. To live each one is to succeed.

—Corita Kent

Never let the fear of striking out get in your way.

—George Herman "Babe" Ruth

When danger approaches, sing to it.

—Arab proverb

All serious daring
starts from within.

—Eudora Welty

Do not try to imitate the lark or the nightingale, if you can't do it. If it's your **destiny** to croak like a toad, then go ahead! And with all your might! Make them hear you!

—Louis-Ferdinand Céline

When you have faults,
do not fear to
abandon them.

—Confucius

I will be small in small things, great among great.

—Pindar

The secret of joy in work
is contained in one word—
excellence. To know how to
do something well is
to enjoy it.

—Pearl Buck

244

Of stealing bases: When you get on first, know you're going to second. Know you can beat the pitcher and the catcher and the two of them combined. You have to have an inner conceit to be a successful base stealer. You have to know you are better than either the pitcher or the catcher.

—Pete Reiser to Maury Wills

Our life is what our thoughts make it.

—Marcus Aurelius

Do not rely completely on any other human being, however dear. We meet all life's greatest tests alone.

—**Agnes Macphail**

Try not to become a man of success but rather try to become a man of value.

—Albert Einstein

The bravest thing you can do when you are not brave is to profess courage and act accordingly.

—Corra Harris

If you have an important point to make, don't try to be subtle or clever. Use a pile driver. Hit the point once. Then come back and hit it again. Then hit it a third time—a tremendous whack.

—Winston Churchill

To be successful, the first thing to do is fall in love with your work.

—Sister Mary Lauretta

251

Hide not your light
under a bushel.

—American proverb

Courage is resistance to fear,
mastery of fear—not
absence of fear.

—Mark Twain

You have to do a little bragging on yourself even to your relations—man doesn't get anywhere without advertising.

—John Nance Garner

A women's organization was the catalyst to trigger a flip-flop in my mind that I wasn't a follower, I was a leader. And in spite of my first reaction, that of fear, and a feeling I couldn't do it, I took the risk. Don't listen to other people's negativity; they filter through their own experiences. Learn to trust your own feelings. If you feel in your gut you have a winner, you have to do it no matter what.

—Ginger Purdy

Get someone else to blow your horn and the sound will carry twice as far.

—Will Rogers

To succeed in any endeavor takes relentless belief in yourself. We have to be committed. We can determine our destiny.

—Willye B. White

The wise man in the storm prays God, not for safety from danger, but for deliverance from fear.

—Ralph Waldo Emerson

Success follows doing what you want to do. There is no other way to be successful.

—Malcolm Forbes

You've got to take the
initiative and play *your* game.
In a decisive set,
confidence is the difference.

—Chris Evert

It's very important to define success for *yourself*. If you really want to reach for the brass ring, just remember that there are sacrifices that go along.

—**Cathleen Black**

Do not divert your attention to the directing minds of others; look straight ahead to where Nature is leading you, to the nature of the Whole through what befalls you, and your own nature through what you must do, for every man must do what is compatible with his own make-up.

—Marcus Aurelius

262

The great man is he who does not lose his child's heart.

—Mencius

You always need to make ideals clear to yourself. You always have to be aware of them, even if there is no direct path to their realization. Were there no **ideals**, there would be no hope whatsoever. Then everything would be hopelessness, darkness—a blind alley.

—Dr. Andrei Sakharov

My mother drew a distinction between achievement and success. She said that achievement is the knowledge that you have studied and worked hard and done the best that is in you. Success is being praised by others, and that's nice, too, but not as important or satisfying. Always aim for achievement and forget about success.

—Helen Hayes

Getting ahead in a difficult profession requires avid faith in yourself. That is why some people with mediocre talent, but with great inner drive, go much further than people with vastly superior talent.

—Sophia Loren

Boys, there ain't no free lunches in this country. And don't go spending your whole life commiserating that you got the raw deals. You've got to say, "I think that if I keep working at this and want it bad enough I can have it." It's called perseverance.

—Lee J. Iacocca

As soon as you trust yourself, you will know how to live.

—Johann Wolfgang von Goethe

Don't accept that others know you better than yourself.

—Sonja Friedman

The only way to enjoy
anything in this life is
to earn it first.

—Ginger Rogers

Power is strength and the ability to see yourself through your own eyes and not through the eyes of another. It is being able to place a circle of power at your own feet and not take power from someone else's circle.

—Lynn V. Andrews

Trust your hopes,
not your fears.

—David Mahoney

Success follows doing what you want to do. There is no other way to be successful.

—Malcolm Forbes

Don't smoke too much, drink too much, eat too much or work too much. We're all on the road to the grave—but there's no reason to be in the passing lane.

—Robert Orben

Success is having a flair for the thing that you are doing; knowing that is not enough, that you have got to have hard work and a certain sense of purpose.

—Margaret Thatcher

275

The way to get things done is not to mind who gets the credit of doing them.

—Benjamin Jowett

It's important to run not on the fast track, but on *your* track. Pretend you have only six months to live. Make three lists: the things you have to do, want to do, and neither have to do nor want to do. Then, for the rest of your life, forget everything in the third category.

—Robert S. Eliot and Dennis L. Breo

. . . Self-esteem isn't everything; it's just that there's nothing without it.

—Gloria Steinem

278

Nothing great was ever
achieved without
enthusiasm.

—Ralph Waldo Emerson

. . . for the joy of life consists largely in the joy of savoring the struggle, whether it ends in success or in failure. Your ability to go through life successfully will depend largely upon your travelling with courage and a good sense of humor, for both are conditions of survival.

—John R. Silber

280

I do not ask to walk smooth paths
nor bear an easy load.
I pray for strength and fortitude
to climb the rock-strewn road.
Give me such courage and I can scale
the hardest peaks alone,
And transform every stumbling block
into a stepping stone.

—Gail Brook Burket

Think wrongly, if you please, but in all cases think for yourself.

—Doris Lessing

Always bear in mind that your own resolution to success is more important than any other one thing.

—Abraham Lincoln

283

Don't listen to those who say, "It's not done that way." Maybe it's not, but maybe you will. Don't listen to those who say, "You're taking too big a chance." Michelangelo would have painted the Sistine floor, and it would surely be rubbed out by today. Most importantly, don't listen when the little voice of fear inside of you rears its ugly head and says, "They're all smarter than you out there. They're more talented, they're taller, blonder, prettier, luckier and have connections . . . " I firmly believe that if you follow a path that interests you, not to the exclusion of love, sensitivity, and cooperation with others, but with the strength of conviction that you can move others by your own efforts, and do not make success or failure the criteria by which you live, the chances are you'll be a person worthy of your own respect.

—Neil Simon

I have no regrets. I wouldn't have lived my life the way I did if I was going to worry about what people were going to say.

—Ingrid Bergman

There is only one success—to be able to spend your life in your own way.

—**Christopher Morley**

286

You must shift your
sail with the wind.

—Italian proverb

I have not ceased being fearful, but I have ceased to let fear control me. I have accepted fear as a part of life—specifically the fear of change, the fear of the unknown; and I have gone ahead despite the pounding in my heart that says: turn back, turn back, you'll die if you venture too far.

—Erica Jong

288

Forgiveness is the
key to action
and freedom.

—Hannah Arendt

You must train your intuition—you must trust that small voice inside you which tells you exactly what to say, what to decide. Your intuition is your instrument. If you can imagine, I throw a spear into the dark. That is my intuition, and then I have to send an expedition into the jungle to find the spear and to find a way to the spear. And that is absolutely another process. That is my intellect.

—Ingmar Bergman

Four steps to achievement:
plan purposefully, prepare
prayerfully, proceed positively,
pursue persistently.

—William A. Ward

What another would have done as well as you, do not do it. What another would have said as well as you, do not say it; what another would have written as well, do not write it. Be faithful to that which exists nowhere but in yourself—and thus make yourself indispensable.

—André Gide

If you don't daydream and kind of plan things out in your imagination, you never get there. So you have to start someplace.

—Robert Duvall

I'd gone through life believing in the strength and competence of others; never in my own. Now, dazzled, I discovered that *my* capacities were real. It was like finding a fortune in the lining of an old coat.

—Joan Mills

Don't look over other people's shoulders. Look in their eyes. Don't talk *at* your children. Take their faces in your hands and talk *to* them. Don't make love to a body, make love to a person.

—Leo Buscaglia

Of course there is no formula for success except, perhaps, an unconditional acceptance of life and what it brings.

—Arthur Rubinstein

If you wish to begin life at forty, you must settle two large personal questions first of all. You must find work and play that call for no more energy than you can afford to spend on them. Then you must train your mind, eye and hand to the point of working and playing with ease, grace and precision.

—Walter B. Pitkin

Never build a case
against yourself.

—Robert Rowbottom

298

Not in the clamor of the
crowded street,
Not in the shouts and plaudits
of the throng,
But in ourselves are triumph
and defeat.

—Henry Wadsworth Longfellow

You are the
product of your
own brainstorm.

—Rosemary Konner Steinbaum

300

When you're afraid, keep your
mind on what you have to do.
And if you have been thoroughly
prepared, you will not be afraid.

—Dale Carnegie

The secret of genius is to carry the spirit of the child into old age, which means never losing your enthusiasm.

—Aldous Huxley

Don't waste your time trying to control the uncontrollable, or trying to solve the unsolvable, or thinking about what could have been. Instead, think about what *can be* if you wisely control what you *can* control and solve the problems you *can* solve with the wisdom you have gained from both your victories and your defeats in the past.

—David Mahoney

Too many people let others stand in their way and don't go back for one more try.

—Rosabeth Moss Kanter

In whatever arena of life one may meet the challenge of courage, whatever may be the sacrifices he faces if he follows his conscience—the loss of his friends, his fortune, his contentment, even the esteem of his fellow men—each man must decide for himself the course he will follow. The stories of past courage can define that ingredient—they can teach, they can offer hope, they can provide inspiration. But they cannot supply courage itself. For this each man must look into his own soul.

— John F. Kennedy

The will to succeed is important, but what's even more important is the will to prepare.

—Bobby Knight

The longer you live and the more you learn, the more clearly you will feel the difference between the few men who are truly great and the mere *virtuosi* . . . I must deny myself the applause of the crowd . . . The point is not to take the world's opinion as a guiding star but to go one's way in life and work unerringly, neither depressed by failure nor seduced by applause. A true "personality" . . . is like a robust organism that, with unconscious sureness, seeks out and digests the nourishment appropriate to it and vigorously rejects that which is unsuitable. You must renounce all superficiality, all convention, all vanity and delusion . . .

—Gustav Mahler

Financial success comes second.
My greatest accomplishment is
raising my children to be caring,
contributing members of the world.

—Caroline Rose Hunt

If you do not hope, you
will not find what is
beyond your hopes.

—St. Clement of Alexandria

We succeed only as we identify in life, or in war, or in anything else, a single overriding objective, and make all other considerations bend to that one objective.

—Dwight D. Eisenhower

Don't fish for strawberries in the bottom of the sea. Never venture anything upon a mere possibility of success; a good probability should always be in view, before we enter upon expense or expose our reputation for any attempt.

—Samuel Palmer

311

It is not always by plugging away at a difficulty and sticking to it that one overcomes it; often it is by working on the one next to it. Some things and some people have to be approached obliquely, at an angle.

—André Gide

Get to know yourself: Know your own failings, passions, and prejudices so you can separate them from what you see. Know also when you actually have thought through to the nature of the thing with which you are dealing and when you are not thinking at all . . . Knowing yourself and knowing the facts, you can judge whether you can change the situation so it is more to your liking. If you cannot—or if you do not know how to improve on things—then discipline yourself to the adjustments that will be necessary.

—**Bernard M. Baruch**

Part III:

The Moderate Approach

Discover day-to-day excitement.

—Charles Baudelaire

I believe that all of us have the capacity for one adventure inside us, but great adventure is facing responsibility day after day.

—William Gordon

Remember your past mistakes just long enough to profit by them.

—Dan McKinnon

You have to accept whatever comes and the only important thing is that you meet it with the best you have to give.

—Eleanor Roosevelt

${\Large A}$rrange whatever
pieces come your way.

—Virginia Woolf

318

Victory is not won in miles but in inches. Win a little now, hold your ground, and later win a little more.

—Louis L'Amour

Keep making the
movements of life.

—Thornton Wilder

If you don't like the way the world is, you change it. You have an obligation to change it. You just do it one step at a time.

—Marian Wright Edelman

Don't evaluate your life in terms of achievements, trivial *or* monumental, along the way. If you do, you will be destined to the frustration of always seeking out other destinations, and never **allowing** yourself actually to be fulfilled . . . Instead, wake up and appreciate everything you encounter along your path. Enjoy the flowers that are there for your pleasure. Tune in to the sunrise, the little children, the laughter, the rain and the birds. Drink it all in . . . *there is no way to happiness; happiness IS the way.*

—Dr. Wayne W. Dyer

Nothing is particularly
hard if you divide it
into small jobs.

—Ray Kroc

One only gets to the top rung on the ladder by steadily climbing up one at a time, and suddenly all sorts of powers, all sorts of abilities which you thought *never* belonged to you— suddenly become within your own possibility and you think, 'Well, I'll have a go, too.'

—**Margaret Thatcher**

The art of life lies in a
constant readjustment to
our surroundings.

—Kakuzo Okakura

Saddle your dreams
afore you ride 'em.

—Mary Webb

Becoming a star may not be
your destiny, but being the
best that you can be is
a goal that you can set
for yourselves.

—Bryan Lindsay

Would that there were an award for people who come to understand the concept of enough. Good enough. Successful enough. Thin enough. Rich enough. Socially responsible enough. When you have self-respect you have enough, and when you have enough, you have self-respect.

—**Gail Sheehy**

328

Sit loosely in the saddle of life.

—Robert Louis Stevenson

329

As you attempt to make big differences, remember to appreciate the small differences. And remember that you don't always have to **reach** the goal you set in order to make a difference. T. H. White, in the last chapter of his story of King Arthur, tells of a discouraged king ready to enter his last battle. His dream of a just society, his roundtable, is destroyed. Then one of his loyal friends, a member of his council . . . tugs on his tunic and reminds him that his effort, his example, has made everything worthwhile.

—Win Borden

Life is an adventure
in forgiveness.

—Norman Cousins

Living is a form of not being sure, not knowing what's next or how. The moment you know how, you begin to die a little.

—Agnes de Mille

Let us follow our destiny,
ebb and flow. Whatever may
happen, we master fortune
by accepting it.

—Virgil

Adventure is something you seek for pleasure, or even for profit, like a gold rush or invading a country; . . . but experience is what really happens to you in the long run; the truth that finally overtakes you.

—Katherine Anne Porter

One of the things your mother wrote you that hit me hard was her advice: "Let go your hold" as Wm. James says, "resign your destiny to higher powers."

—Agnes Meyer to Adlai E. Stevenson

If your head tells you one thing and your heart tells you another, before you do anything, you should first decide whether you have a better head or a better heart.

—Marilyn Vos Savant

No great thing is created suddenly.

—Epictetus

The best things are nearest—breath in your nostrils, light in your eyes, flowers at your feet, duties at your hand, the path of Right just before you. Do not grasp at the stars, but do life's plain common work as it comes, certain that daily duties and daily bread are the sweetest things in life.

—Robert Louis Stevenson

Slow and steady
wins the race.

—Aesop

You've got to decide on an inner discipline to protect yourself. Step out of the interesting, dynamic rhythm every so often and focus on your internal life. Say "Stop the world, I want to get off" for a while at least.

—Naomi Rosenblatt

Learn by practice. Whether it means to learn to dance by practicing dancing or to live by practicing living, the principles are the same. In each, it is the performance of the dedicated precise set of acts, physical or intellectual, from which comes shape of achievement, a sense of one *being*, a satisfaction. One becomes, in some area, an athlete of God.

—Martha Graham

Take calculated risks.
That is quite different from
being rash.

—George S. Patton

Mighty oaks from little acorns grow.

—Saying

Part IV:
Facing Adversity

Oh, we all get run over—once in
our lives. But one must pick
oneself up again. And behave
as if it were nothing.

—Henrik Ibsen

A man's life is interesting primarily when he has failed— I well know. For it is a sign that he tried to surpass himself.

—Georges Clemenceau

'Tis not the softer things of life

Which stimulate man's will to strive;

But bleak adversity and strife

Do most to keep man's will alive.

O'er rose-strewn paths the
weaklings creep,

But brave hearts dare to
climb the steep.

—Anonymous

We become wiser by adversity; prosperity destroys our appreciation of the right.

—Seneca the Younger

Hardships and handicaps can . . . stimulate our energy to survive them. You'll find if you study the lives of people who've accomplished things, it's often been done with the help of great willpower in overcoming this and that.

—Beatrice Wood

348

Aim for success, NOT perfection." Never give up your right to be wrong, because then you will lose the ability to learn new things and to move forward with your life. Remember that fear always lurks behind perfectionism . . . Confronting your fears and allowing yourself the right to be human can, paradoxically, make you a far happier and more productive person.

—Dr. David M. Burns

Do not . . . hope wholly to reason away your troubles; do not feed them with attention, and they will die imperceptibly away. Fix your thoughts upon your business, fill your intervals with company, and sunshine will again break in upon your mind.

—Samuel Johnson

You may be
disappointed if you fail,
but you are doomed
if you don't try.

—Beverly Sills

Never confuse a single defeat with a final defeat.

—F. Scott Fitzgerald

Whenever you fall, pick something up.

—Oswald Avery

Show me a person who has never made a mistake and I'll show you somebody who has never achieved much.

—Joan Collins

Stumbling is
not falling.

—Portuguese proverb

You must accept that you might fail; then, if you do your best and still don't win, at least you can be satisfied that you've tried. If you don't **accept** failure as a possibility, you don't set high goals, you don't branch out, you don't try—you don't take the risk.

—Rosalynn Carter

In the cellars of the night, when the mind starts moving around old trunks of bad times, the pain of this and the shame of that, the memory of a small boldness is a hand to hold.

—John Leonard

The only people who never fail are those who never try.

—Ilka Chase

First ask yourself: What is the worst that can happen? Then prepare to accept it. Then proceed to improve on the worst.

—Dale Carnegie

Our greatest glory is not in
never falling but in rising
every time we fall.

—Confucius

When we can begin to take our failures nonseriously, it means we are ceasing to be afraid of them. It is of immense importance to learn to laugh at ourselves.

—Katherine Mansfield

They say you can't do it,
but remember, that
doesn't always work.

—Casey Stengel

It is no sin to attempt and fail. The only sin is not to make the attempt.

—SuEllen Fried

Let us be of good cheer,
remembering that the
misfortunes hardest to bear
are those that
will never happen.

—James Russell Lowell

How you handle defeat is not something to be taken lightly. You've got to think it through. Defeat is an art form. You've got to accept it, and you've got to go on. And once you do that, it's not bad.

—Walter F. Mondale

365

The greater the difficulty, the greater the glory.

—Cicero

We are not interested in the possibilities of defeat.

—Queen Victoria

Everybody can be great . . . because anybody can serve. You don't have to have a college degree to serve. You don't have to make your subject and verb agree to serve. You only need a heart full of grace. A soul generated by love.

—Martin Luther King, Jr.

Accept the challenges,
so that you may feel the
exhilaration of victory.

—George Patton

Lord, grant that I may
always desire more than
I can accomplish.

—Michelangelo

Success is to be measured
not so much by the position that
one has reached in life as by the
obstacles which he has overcome
while trying to succeed.

—Booker T. Washington

Fire tries gold,
misfortune men.

—Anonymous

Unless you try to do something beyond what you have already mastered, you will never grow.

—Ronald E. Osborn

This book was set in Bodoni Book and

Poster Bodoni Compressed

by Barbara M. Bachman.

Book design by Judith Stagnitto Abbate

Cover design by Sara Stemen